Young Women of Faith

Hey!

This is Me

Other books in the Young Women of Faith Library

Fiction:
Here's Lily
Lily Robbins, M.D. (Medical Dabbler)
Lily and the Creep
Lily's Ultimate Party
Ask Lily
Lily the Rebel

Non-fiction:
The Beauty Book
The Body Book
The Buddy Book
The Best Bash Book
The Blurry Rules Book
The It's MY Life Book

Dear Diary: A Girl's Book of Devotions
Girlz Want to Know: Answers to Real-Life Questions

Young Women of Faith

Hey!

This is Me

Written by Connie Neal
Illustrated by Casey Neal

Zonderkidz

This book was created with the
help and good ideas of
Haley Neal (9)
and
Sarah Flower (11).

Thanks, girls!

~CN

Hey!

This Is Your Book!

The great thing about this book is that you get to do it your way. When this book is done, there will never ever be another like it anywhere because **you** are the author, and there is no one else like you.

You are what makes this book special. In fact, God thinks you are so special that he has already written about you in his book, the Bible. In Psalm 139, it says that God knows all about you. God knows exactly how many days you will live your life on earth. Each day of your life is so important to God that he wrote that number in his book. That same chapter says that God knows and cares about what is in your HEART, what you are thinking, what you are doing every minute, day and night.

God *cares* about what is going on inside you and what you have to say. When you pour out your heart to God, he **pays attention!** Since all these things about you are important enough to go in God's book, they are important enough to go in your book too!

A Word about Writing

Many people get **nervous** about writing. Think of writing as talking on paper. You don't get nervous about talking, do you? If you just remind yourself that writing is only talking on paper, you will actually **enjoy** writing your book. The way you write is up to you. You may even want to use *poetry* if you have that talent.

Some books are all words. Some use words and pictures. Feel free to use both. You can **express** your thoughts about what you did or what you dream of doing or becoming in a picture or a cartoon. You can also explain it in words. Write about what's important to you and add illustrations, or picture something and add a few words or the date as a caption to the picture. Use your own special **style** to think, write, and draw in your journal. Relax and express yourself! There's lots of room to describe what's going on in your life. In these pages you can…

Talk to God and write down answers to your prayers.

Keep track of your good friends.

Wish and wonder and dream.

Plan your future.

Think about things that matter to you.

Collect a list of things you like.

Tell about your life as you see it now.

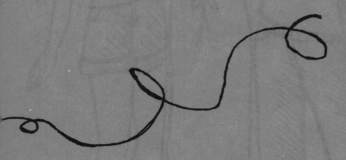

Develop your talents—
writing, drawing, coloring, thinking, and planning.

Keep secrets.

Add anything else you want!

FAMILY
AND FRIENDS

Family and friends
are an important part of your
life. God uses family relation-
ships to give you the chance to be
loved and to learn to love other people. Friends make life happier.
Friends give you the opportunity to
learn to get along with other people. To have lots of friends,
you need to be friendly
to others.

Everyone needs friends.

Perfume and incense bring joy to your heart. And friends are sweeter when they give you honest advice. Don't desert your friends.

Proverbs 27:9-10

Two people are better than one. They can help each other in everything they do. Suppose someone falls down. Then a friend can help him up. But suppose the one who falls down doesn't have anyone to help him up. Then feel sorry for him!

Ecclesiastes 4:9-10

God said, "Honor your father and mother."

Matthew 15:4

Dear friends,
since God loved
us that much, we
should also love one
another.

1 John 4:11

Friends love at all times.
They are there to help
when trouble comes.

Proverbs 17:17

My
Notes:

_____

_____

_____

_____

_____

_____

_____

_____

_____

_____

Draw a **picture** of **your** family

Write how you feel about **each** person

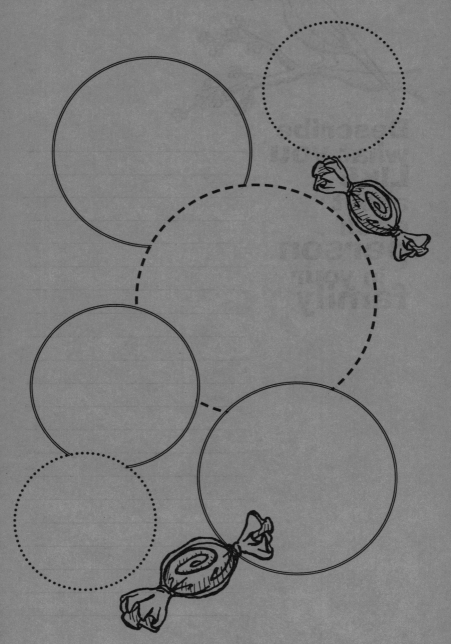

Describe
what **you**
Lᴉᴋᴇ
about
each
person
in your
family

_____
_____
_____
_____
_____
_____
_____
_____
_____
_____
_____
_____
_____
_____
_____
_____
_____
_____
_____
_____
_____
_____

Write about conflicts you have with brothers and sisters

_____
_____
_____
_____
_____
_____
_____
_____
_____
_____
_____
_____
_____
_____

_____   _____
_____   _____
_____   _____
_____   _____
_____   _____

_____   _____
_____   _____
_____   _____
_____   _____
_____   _____

_____   _____
_____   _____
_____   _____

Then list ideas about how you can work out your problems nicely

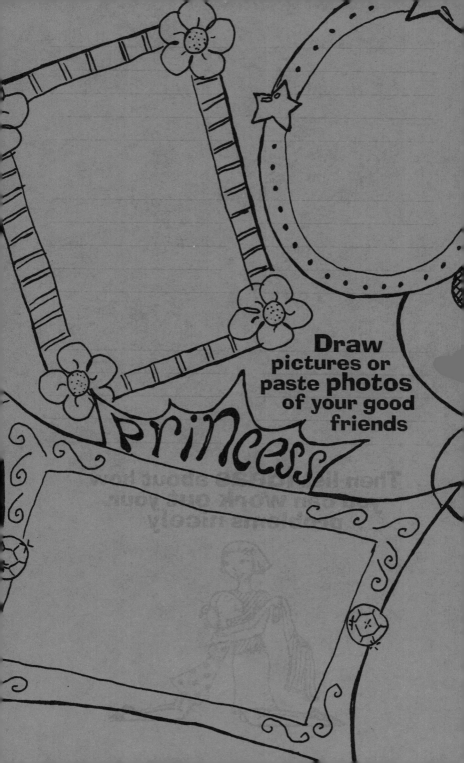

**Draw
pictures or
paste photos
of your good
friends**

princess

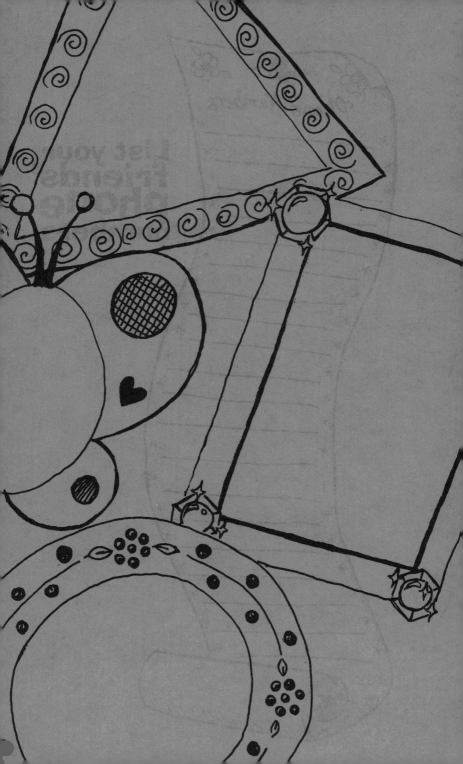

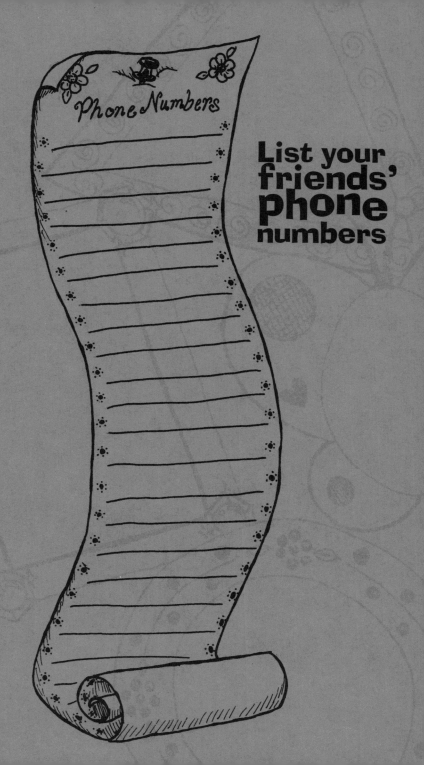

List your friends' phone numbers

name: _____

address: _____

phone: _____

email: _____

name: _____

address: _____

phone: _____

email: _____

name: _____

address: _____

phone: _____

email: _____

name: _____

address: _____

phone: _____

email: _____

Keep addresses
for relatives who
live somewhere else

Plan parties or outings you want
to have with your family or friends

Whatever else you want to add about family or friends!

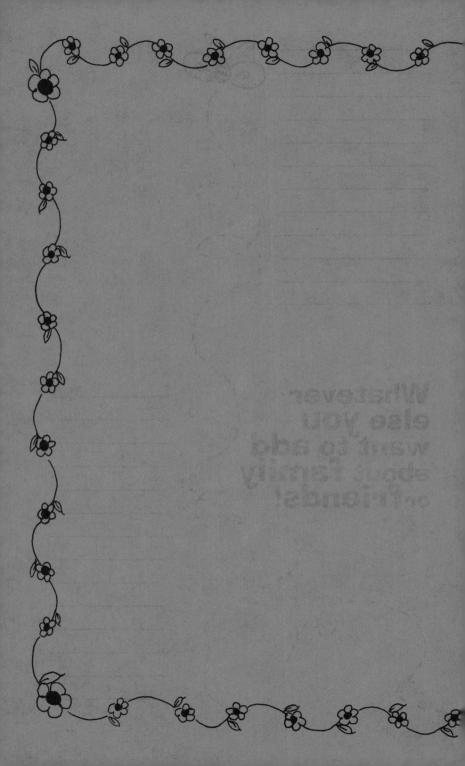

WHAT'S HAPPENING?

This section is where you can record what is happening in your life. This is the place to put things you are DOING.

"They will tell you everything that is happening here."

Colossians 4:9

Things you have done

_____
_____
_____
_____
_____
_____
_____
_____
_____
_____
_____
_____
_____
_____
_____
_____
_____
_____
_____
_____

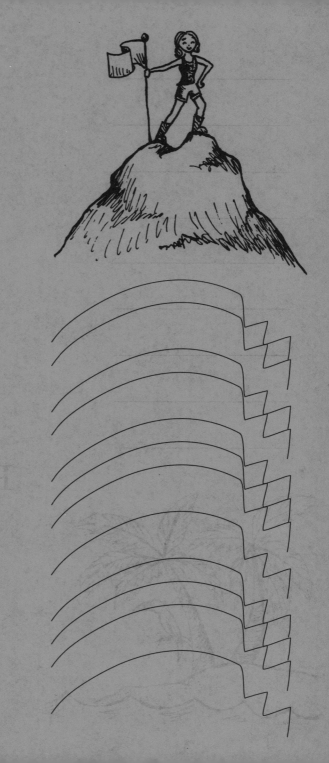

_____

_____

_____

_____

_____

_____

_____

Places
you
have
been

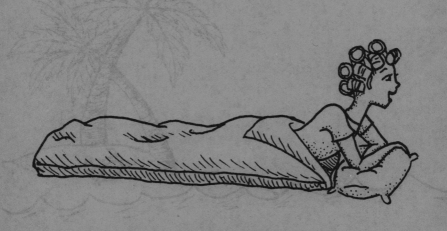

Special
events

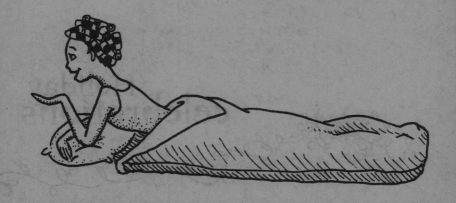

Holiday
celebrations

What is happening

at school

Things
your
family is
doing

_____

_____

_____

_____

_____

_____

_____

_____

_____

_____

_____

_____

_____

_____

_____

_____

_____

_____

_____

_____

_____

_____

_____

_____

_____

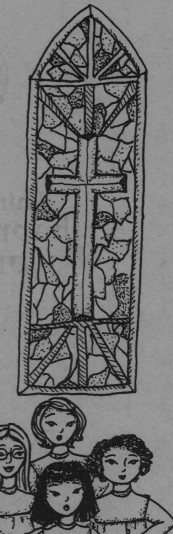

Things you
are doing
at church

Things that are happening in the world around you

(ruled writing lines)

How I am Feeling

God knows and
cares about all your feelings.
God is happy when you are filled
with joy. God is near you when you
feel so sad you think your heart might
break. One verse even says that God saves
your tears in a bottle! You can tell God all your
feelings—even the ones that people may not like
to deal with.

Feelings are not right or wrong. But some emotions
sure feel better than others! And some feelings can lead
to doing things that are wrong. So it is good to know
how you are feeling. It helps to get your feelings out in
ways that don't hurt others. If you are angry, you can
write out what you are thinking instead of saying it to
someone it might hurt. You can draw pictures that show
your feelings. You may be red with anger or green with
envy or so sad you are feeling blue.

This section is your place to pour out your heart to
God. It is your place to put your feelings on paper. It
will help you sort out what you are feeling and why.
Even though you feel deeply, your life doesn't have
to be ruled by feelings. You can choose to get rid
of anger and bitterness. You can choose a cheer-
ful attitude when you are having a bad day.
You can have joy in life even though you
sometimes feel sad. But knowing what
you are feeling is the place to start.
So go ahead and talk about
your feelings here.

God knows and _____ about all your feelings.
God is happy when you are filled
with joy. God is near you when you
feel sad and you think your heart might
break. (Onyx verse) can save that God saves
your tears in a bottle. God can tell God your
feelings — even the ones that people may not like
to deal with.

_____ are not right or wrong. But some emotions
can lead to actions that others. And some feelings can lead
_____ you know when your feelings are wrong? Learning to know
how you feel and putting this together and feelings out in
_____ the difference. (If) your anger can run
wild out what you are feeling then talk God or praying it to
someone. _____ might keep from doing things that show
your feelings. You might _____ how you treat others with
anger or so you are feeling sad.

_____ section is a safe place to put down your heart to you.
_____ it is possible to put your feelings on paper. It
will help you to _____ what When you have finished with
Even though you feel deeply. When the feelings come?
_____ the links. You can (choose) what to
of anger and the devil. You can choose... the
ful attitude when you are but you had it now.
You can have joys like even though you
sometimes feel sad. But following what
_____ is the plan to start.
go ahead and talk about
your feelings...

Jesus was full of joy through the Holy Spirit. Luke 10:21

Jesus sobbed. John 11:35

The LORD is close to those whose hearts have been broken. He saves those whose spirits have been crushed. Psalm 34:18

When you are angry, do not sin. Do not let the sun go down while you are still angry. Don't give the devil a chance. Ephesians 4:26

Write down my poem of sadness. List my tears on your scroll. Aren't you making a record of them? Psalm 56:8

I will be glad and full of joy because you love me. You saw that I was hurting. You took note of my great pain. Psalm 31:7

Are any of you in trouble? Then you should pray. Are any of you happy? Then sing songs of praise. James 5:13

Be joyful with those who are joyful. Be sad with those who are sad. Romans 12:15

Describe feelings
guilty about
something you
did wrong

Describe
how you
feel

Describe feeling
guilty about
something YOU
did wrong

_____
_____
_____
_____
_____
_____
_____
_____
_____
_____
_____
_____
_____
_____
_____
_____
_____
_____
_____
_____

_____
_____
_____
_____
_____
_____
_____
_____
_____
_____
_____
_____
_____
_____
_____

Describe how YOU feel when you are

disappointed

Describe the things you feel grateful for

(and give thanks to God)

_____
_____
_____
_____
_____
_____
_____
_____
_____
_____
_____
_____
_____
_____
_____
_____
_____

Write your
feelings
out to God as
a prayer

THiNGS I LiKE

This is the section where you collect things you like. You can describe the kinds of things you like. You can make lists of things you like. You can draw pictures of things you like. Or you can cut pictures out of magazines and glue them into the pages. This is the place to record your FAVORITE things.

I will praise the LORD.
I won't forget anything he does for me.
He forgives all my sins.
He heals all my sicknesses.
He saves my life from going down into the grave.
His faithful and tender love makes me feel like a king.
He satisfies me with the good things I long for.
Then I feel young and strong again, just like an eagle.

Psalm 103:2-5

My
Notes:

_____
_____
_____
_____
_____
_____
_____
_____

Things you like to do

Things
you like
to eat

Your favorite Bible verses

Your favorite music or music artist

Your favorite TV shows

Movies you like

_____
_____
_____
_____
_____
_____
_____
_____
_____
_____
_____
_____
_____
_____
_____
_____
_____
_____
_____

The
kinds
of
clothes
you
like

The kinds of hair-styles you like

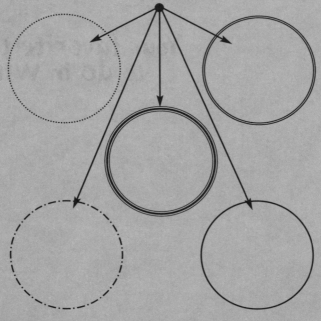

Your favorite things to do in winter

or summer

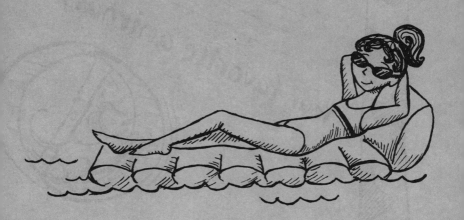

Your favorite animals.

Games you like to play

Your favorite
things to
collect

I Wonder...

There are many things that you may wonder about. It's good to wonder. Use this section to take note of anything that makes you wonder. As you grow up, you may learn things that explain the things you wondered about.

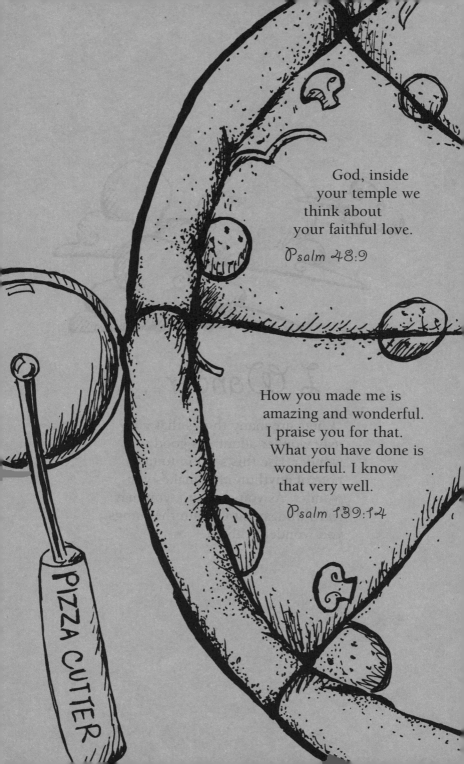

God, inside
your temple we
think about
your faithful love.

Psalm 48:9

How you made me is
amazing and wonderful.
I praise you for that.
What you have done is
wonderful. I know
that very well.

Psalm 139:14

PIZZA CUTTER

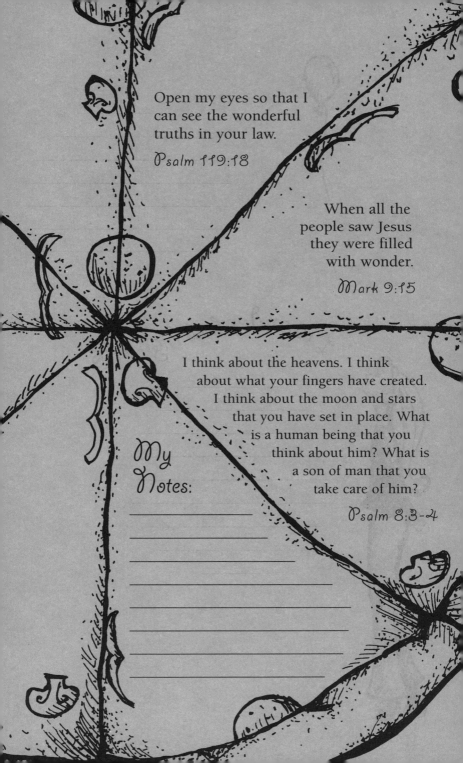

Open my eyes so that I can see the wonderful truths in your law.

Psalm 119:18

When all the people saw Jesus they were filled with wonder.

Mark 9:15

I think about the heavens. I think about what your fingers have created. I think about the moon and stars that you have set in place. What is a human being that you think about him? What is a son of man that you take care of him?

Psalm 8:3-4

My Notes:

_____
_____
_____
_____
_____
_____
_____
_____

_____

_____

_____

_____

_____

_____

_____

I wonder how high is up.

_____

_____

_____

_____

_____

_____

_____

meow

I wonder if cats understand
what other cats are saying
when they meow.

I wonder why people act the way they do.

I wonder how many stars are in the sky.

_____

_____

_____

_____

_____

_____

_____

_____

_____

_____

_____

_____

_____

_____

I wonder what it was
like to live at another
time in history.

I wonder what I will do
when I grow up.

I wonder what heaven will be like.

Anything that follows the words "I wonder . . ." in your mind

I WISH...
(Hopes & Dreams)

People wish and hope and dream all the time. This section is where you can write down or draw pictures of the things you wish for. Some wishes are wild—like wishing it would rain chocolate drops. You can have some fun writing those wishes in this section. Some wishes could come true even though they may take a long time—like wishing you could become an astronaut. Put those in here too. All of your wishes, hopes, and dreams are worth writing down. Then you can choose which of them you will try to make come true with God's help.

Find your delight in the
LORD. Then he will
give you everything your
heart really wants.

Psalm 37:4

Keep me going as you
have promised...Don't let
me lose all hope.

Psalm 119:116

My Notes:

_____
_____
_____
_____
_____
_____
_____

Jesus said to his disciples, "If you remain joined to me and my words remain in you, ask for anything you wish. And it will be given to you."

John 15:7

Hope that can be seen is no hope at all. Who hopes for what is already there? We hope for what we don't have yet. So we are patient as we wait for it.

Romans 8:24

Your wild
wishes

that are fun
to think
about

_____

_____

_____

_____

_____

_____

_____

_____

_____

_____

_____

_____

_____

_____

_____

_____

_____

_____

_____

_____

_____

_____

_____

_____

_____

_____

_____

_____

_____

_____

_____

_____

_____

More wild
wishes

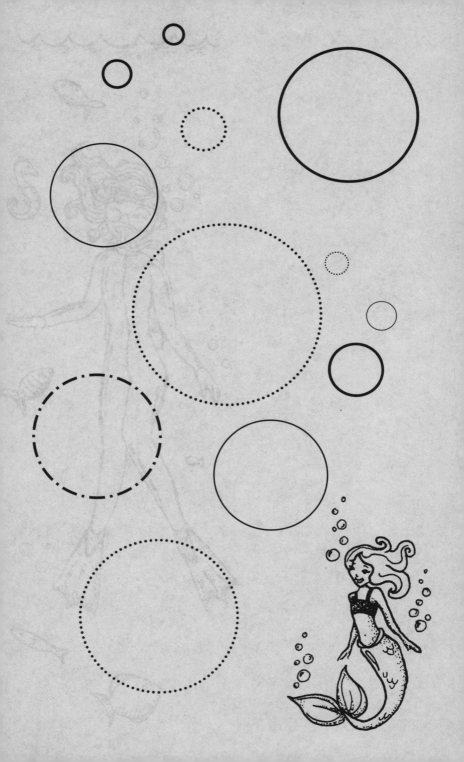

Your
hopes for
yourself
and...

...the
people
you love

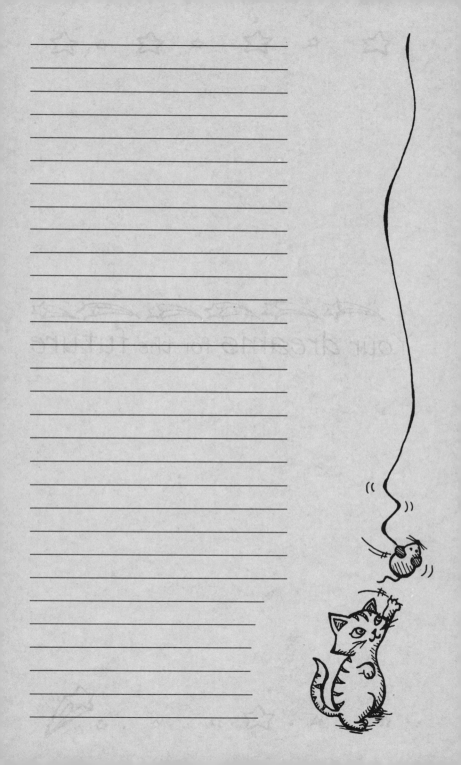

our dreams for the future

Your dreams for the future

I WAS THINKING...

God made you able to think. You can choose the kinds of things you think about. God wants you to choose good things. But there are a lot of things to think about that are not so good. Lots of things you may see on TV or hear may not be good. So you need to keep a list of good things to think about. You can do that in this section.

My eyes stay open
all night long. I spend
my time thinking about
your promises.

Psalm 119:148

My Notes:

Don't think about how to satisfy what our sinful nature wants.
Romans 13:14

The Lord said, "I know what you are thinking."
Ezekiel 11:5

Always think about what is true. Think about what is noble, right and pure. Think about what is lovely and worthy of respect. If anything is excellent or worthy of praise, think about those kinds of things.
Philippians 4:8

Jesus replied, " 'Love the Lord your God with all your heart and with all your soul. Love him with all your mind.' This is the first and most important commandment."
Matthew 22:37

God's promises

you can **think** about

_____

_____

_____

_____

_____

_____

_____

_____

_____

_____

Thinking about how to solve your problems...

...in a **good** way

Inventions
you might
make some day

How they would work.

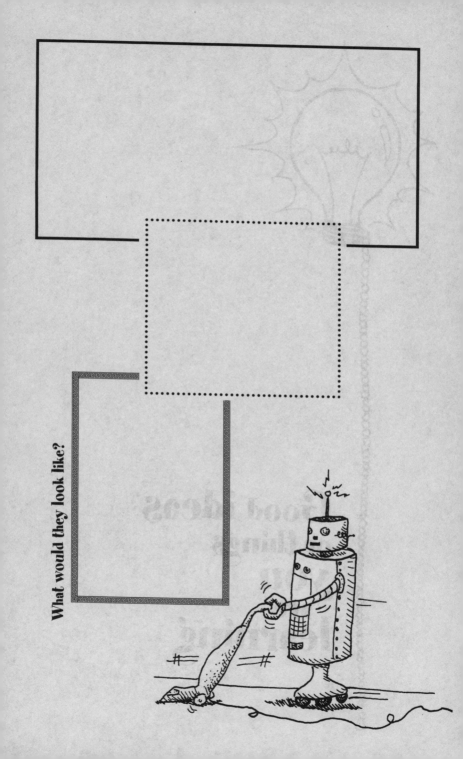

What would they look like?

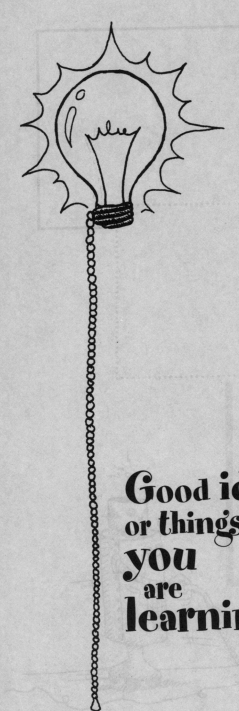

Good ideas or things you are learning

More good ideas or things you are learning

More good ideas or things you are learning

Thinking about how much

Thinking about

God

loves

you

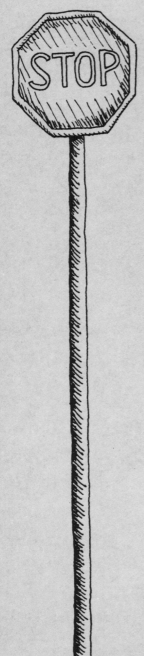

Thinking about

God's directions

for living

Things I Will Do

One of the greatest gifts God gave you is the freedom to choose what you will do. You have a mind that you use to think. You have emotions that cause you to feel. You also have a will that allows you to choose. God wants you to choose to do what is good. There are more good things to do than anyone could do in a lifetime. You get to choose what you will do. God will help you whenever you choose to do something good—even if it is hard. What you choose to do can change how you feel and what happens in your future. This section is where you can write the things you determine you will do—with God's help.

LORD, teach me to
follow your orders.
Then I will obey them to
the very end. Help me
understand your law. Then
I will follow it and obey it
with all my heart.

Psalm 119:33–34

I said, "I will be
careful about how I
live. I will not sin by
what I say."

Psalm 39:1

I will give thanks to the LORD
because he does what is
right. I will sing praise to
the LORD Most High.

Psalm 7:17

Zacchaeus stood up. He
said, "Look, Lord! Here and
now I give half of what I own to
those who are poor. And if I have
cheated anybody out of anything,
I will pay it back.
I will pay back four times
the amount I took."

Luke 19:8

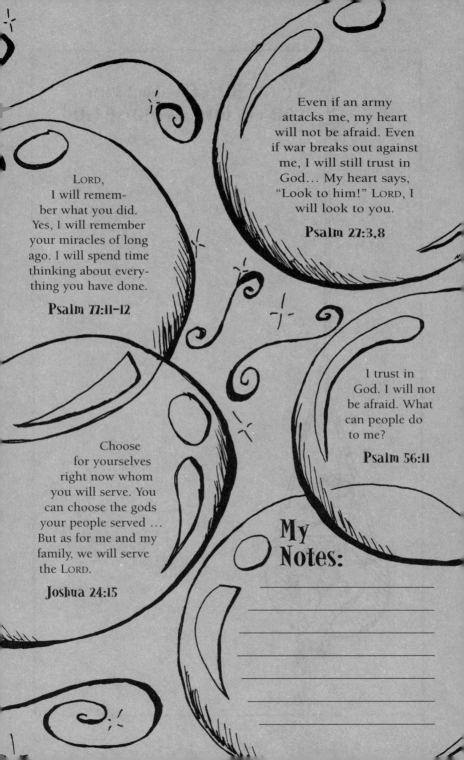

Even if an army attacks me, my heart will not be afraid. Even if war breaks out against me, I will still trust in God… My heart says, "Look to him!" LORD, I will look to you.

Psalm 27:3,8

LORD, I will remember what you did. Yes, I will remember your miracles of long ago. I will spend time thinking about everything you have done.

Psalm 77:11-12

I trust in God. I will not be afraid. What can people do to me?

Psalm 56:11

Choose for yourselves right now whom you will serve. You can choose the gods your people served … But as for me and my family, we will serve the LORD.

Joshua 24:15

My Notes:

_____
_____
_____
_____
_____
_____

Your **choices** about how **you** will love and praise God

Your choices about how you will live

Your goals
and things
you will do

Your

plans

Your promises
of things you
will do around
your house

_____

_____

_____

_____

_____

_____

_____

_____

Your choices about
the things you will not do
(because they are wrong)

_____

_____

_____

_____

_____

_____

_____

_____

A list of
good things
YOU
want to do
sometime
in your life

_____

_____

_____

_____

_____

_____

_____

_____

_____

_____

_____

_____

_____

_____

DeAr GOD...

A Place
for Your Prayers

God wants to hear from you! Praying is talking to God. Putting some of your prayers in this book is like writing God a letter. And God is paying attention! He doesn't want you to be religious when you pray. He just wants you to come to him. You can tell God anything, and you can always ask for his help. God always answers prayers. Sometimes he answers by giving you the things you asked for. Sometimes he answers by making you strong enough to handle your problems. Sometimes he does miracles. Sometimes he gives you good ideas to help you live differently. Sometimes God answers prayers by saying no.

Jesus taught his disciples how to pray like he did. Jesus said in Matthew 6:9-13, "This is how you should pray. 'Our Father in heaven, may your name be honored. May your kingdom come. May what you want to happen be done on earth as it is done in heaven. Give us today our daily bread. Forgive us our sins, just as we also have forgiven those who sin against us. Keep us from falling into sin when we are tempted. Save us from the evil one.'" This is a good prayer to pray anytime.

You can also make up your own prayers.

My Notes

_____
_____
_____
_____
_____
_____

Jesus said, "Love your enemies. Pray for those who hurt you." **Matthew 5:44**

The Lord said, "Then you will call out to me. You will come and pray to me. And I will listen to you. When you look for me with all your heart, you will find me." **Jeremiah 29:12**

God, I call out to you because you will answer me. Listen to me. Hear my prayer. **Psalm 17:6**

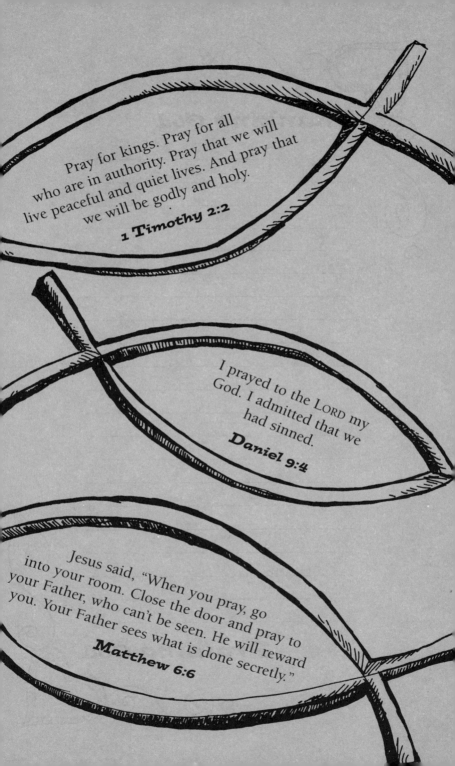

Pray for kings. Pray for all who are in authority. Pray that we will live peaceful and quiet lives. And pray that we will be godly and holy.

1 Timothy 2:2

I prayed to the LORD my God. I admitted that we had sinned.

Daniel 9:4

Jesus said, "When you pray, go into your room. Close the door and pray to your Father, who can't be seen. He will reward you. Your Father sees what is done secretly."

Matthew 6:6

Thanking God

_____

_____

_____

_____

_____

_____

_____

_____

_____

_____

_____

_____

_____

_____

_____

_____

_____

_____

_____

_____

Praising God

_____
_____
_____
_____
_____
_____
_____

Asking **God**
to give you
what you
need

_____
_____
_____
_____
_____
_____

_____
_____
_____
_____
_____
_____

Confessing your sins when you do something wrong

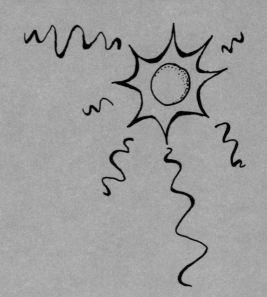

Asking God to forgive you

Expressing
your
feelings
to
God

Telling God
**any-
thing you**
want

Asking God
for
wisdom

Asking God for help when you are in trouble

Asking God to
help you understand
things you don't
understand

_____
_____
_____
_____
_____
_____
_____
_____
_____
_____
_____
_____
_____
_____
_____
_____
_____
_____
_____
_____
_____
_____

Asking **God** to **bless** the **people** you **love**

_____

_____

_____

_____

_____

_____

_____

_____

_____

_____

_____

_____

_____

_____

_____

_____

_____

_____

Asking **God** to **bless** your enemies

Asking God to use you to help others

_____
_____
_____
_____
_____
_____
_____
_____
_____
_____
_____
_____
_____
_____
_____
_____
_____
_____
_____
_____
_____
_____
_____
_____

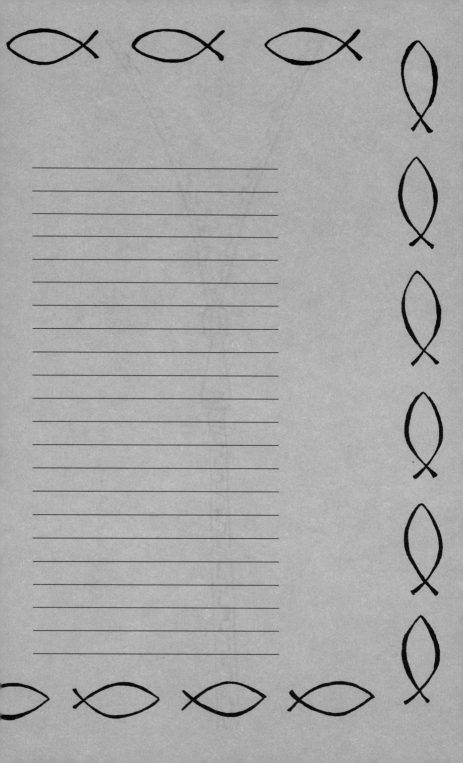

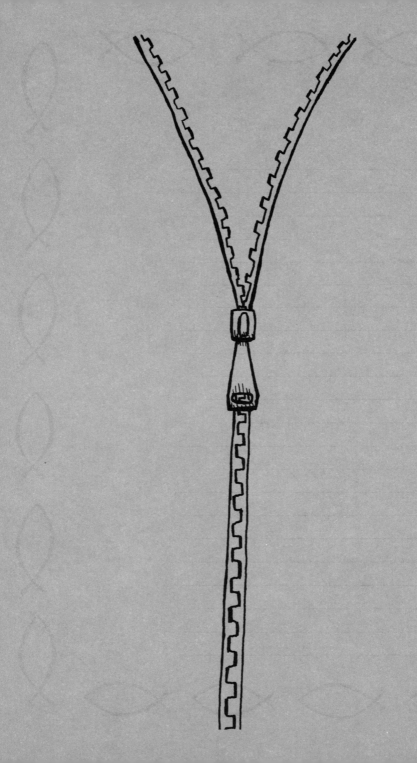

ANSWERS TO MY PRAYERS

When you pray, you are not
just talking to yourself. God is listening.
And God is mighty powerful! God can do
anything. God cares about you. God wants to
be a real part of your life. So when you pray, look
to see how God answers you. When you notice
that God answered a prayer, thank him. Tell people how God answers your prayers. That can help
them trust in God. Look back at how God
answered your prayers. This can help your
faith in God to grow as you grow up. Then
you will not only grow up to be a nice
young lady, you will grow up to be a
real Woman of Faith!

When I'm in
trouble, I will call
out to you.
And you will
answer me.

Psalm 86:7

God, I call
out to you
because you
will answer me.
Listen to me.
Hear my prayer.

Psalm 17:6

We prayed
o our God about all
of those matters.
And he answered
our prayers.

Ezra 8:23

After that,
God answered
prayer and
blessed
the land.

2 Samuel
21:14

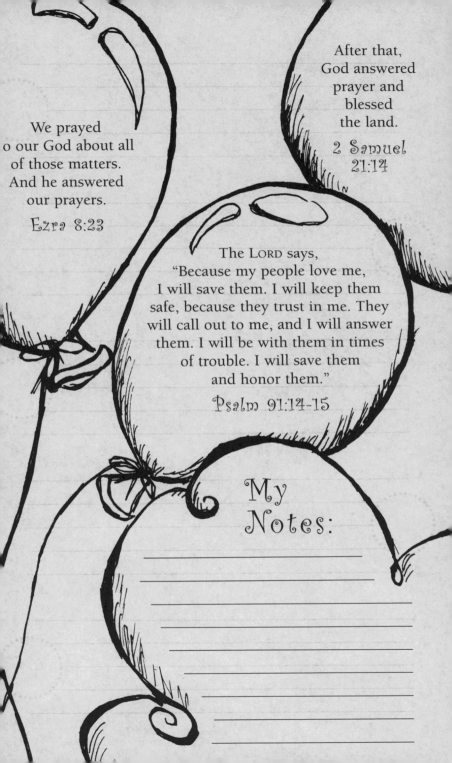

The LORD says,
"Because my people love me,
I will save them. I will keep them
safe, because they trust in me. They
will call out to me, and I will answer
them. I will be with them in times
of trouble. I will save them
and honor them."

Psalm 91:14-15

My
Notes:

Answers to your prayers and the dates they were answered

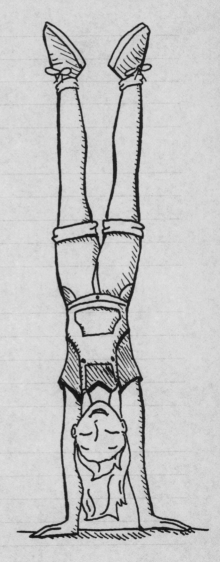

Answers to your
prayers and
the dates they
were answered

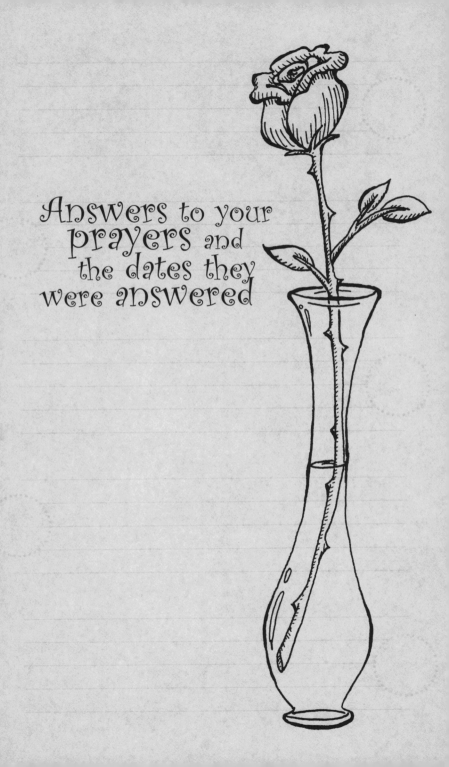

Answers to your
prayers and
the dates they
were answered

Answers to your
prayers and
the dates they
were answered

Thank you notes
to God for
answering
your prayers

Thank you notes to God for answering your prayers

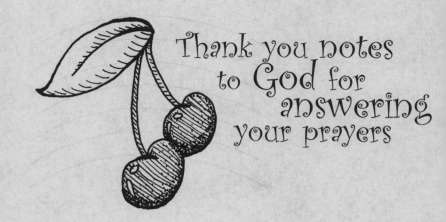

Thank you notes
to God for
answering
your prayers

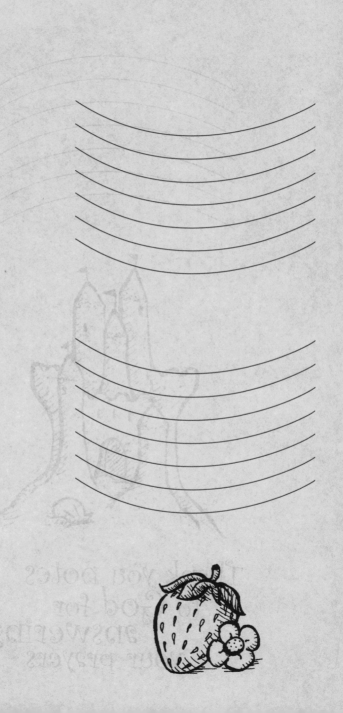

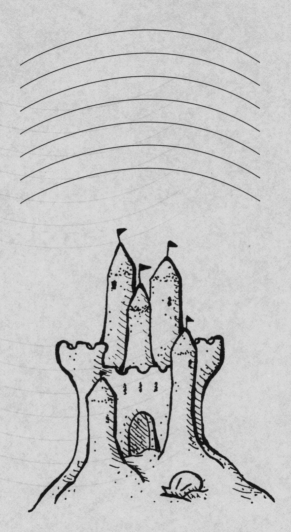

Thank you notes
to God for
answering
your prayers

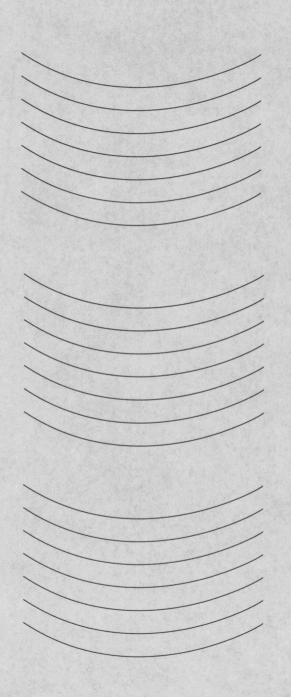

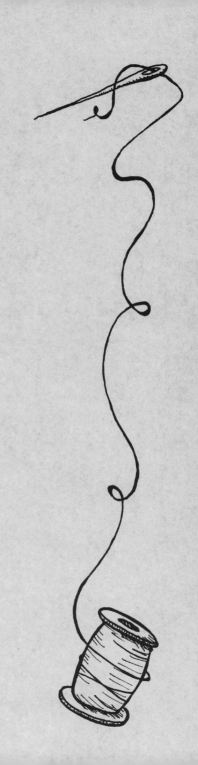

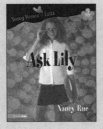
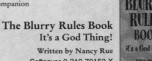

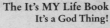

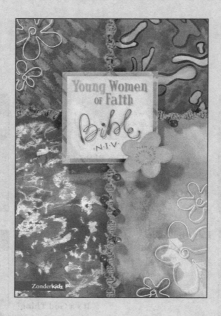

NIV Young Women of Faith Bible
GENERAL EDITOR SUSIE SHELLENBERGER

Designed just for girls ages 8-12, the *NIV Young Women of Faith Bible* not only has a trendy, cool look, it's packed with fun to read in-text features that spark interest, provide insight, highlight key foundational portions of Scripture, and more. Discover how to apply God's word to your everyday life with the *NIV Young Women of Faith Bible.*

Hardcover 0-310-91394-2
Softcover 0-310-70278-X

Zonderkidz™

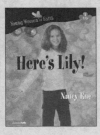